PHILOSOPHERS OF THE SPIRIT

KIERKEGAARD

PHILOSOPHERS OF THE SPIRIT

KIERKEGAARD

Edited by
Robert Van de Weyer

Hodder & Stoughton
LONDON SYDNEY AUCKLAND

First published in Great Britain 1997.

The right of Robert Van de Weyer to be identified as the Editor of this
Work has been asserted by him in accordance with the
Copyright, Designs and Patents Act 1988.

1 3 5 7 9 10 8 6 4 2

British Library Cataloguing in Publication Data:
A record for this book is available from the British Library.

ISBN 0 340 69404 1

Typeset in Monotype Columbus by
Strathmore Publishing Services, London N7.

Printed and bound in Great Britain by
Mackays of Chatham PLC, Chatham, Kent

Hodder and Stoughton Ltd,
A division of Hodder Headline PLC
338 Euston Road, London NW1 3BH

CONTENTS

SERIES INTRODUCTION

The first task of philosophers is to ask questions – the questions which lurk in all our minds, but which, out of fear or confusion, we fail to articulate. Thus philosophers disturb us. The second task of philosophers is to try and answer the questions they have asked. But since their answers are inevitably only partial, philosophers both interest and infuriate us. Their third and most important task is to stimulate and inspire us to ask questions and seek answers for ourselves.

The human psyche or spirit has always been the main – although not the only – focus of philosophy. And inevitably when the psyche is explored, the gap between religion and philosophy rapidly narrows. Indeed for philosophers in the more distant past there was no gap at all, since philosophy was an aspect of theology and even mysticism. Although religious institutions are now quite weak, questions of spiritual philosophy are being asked more keenly and urgently than ever.

This series is an invitation to readers, with no philosophical training whatever, to grapple with the great philosophers of the spirit. Most philosophy nowadays is served in the form of brief summaries, written by commentators. Each of these books contains an introduction to the life and ideas of the philosopher in question. But thereafter the reader encounters the philosopher's original words – translated into modern English. Usually the words are easy to follow; sometimes they are more difficult. They are never dull, always challenging, and frequently entertaining.

INTRODUCTION

His Genius

Søren Kierkegaard is the philosopher for an age when objective religious belief is for most people extremely difficult, if not impossible, but when most people still yearn for some kind of faith. This age began in the nineteenth century, when he was alive, and as the third millennium approaches, shows no sign of ending. He also spoke to a time when the paradox of freedom and determinism, which had always been a theological problem, acquired scientific and psychological dimensions. Again this age continues to the present day; and with the increase in our understanding of genes, and their influence on human personality and behaviour, the paradox becomes ever more acute. Kierkegaard was not an easy writer; his arguments are complex, his logic often tortuous and prone to unexpected leaps, and his prose frequently repetitive. So it is a measure of his continuing and increasing relevance that interest in his work is greater now than ever before.

He had no doubt that religious propositions of any kind could never be objectively proven. More importantly, he contended that, even if they could be proven, this would not in itself make people more likely to accept them. To the chagrin of traditional theologians, he asserted that Christianity, as taught and embodied by Jesus Christ, was never about objective truth. On the contrary, religion in general, and Christianity in particular, are subjective: they are concerned with the subjective transformation of the individual. Objective religion makes a sharp distinction between the knower and that which may be known – between subject and object. And the purpose of objective religion is to enable the subject to know certain objects, most notably God. Subjective religion by contrast is about the relationship between subject and object, between the human being and God; and in that relationship the distinction disappears. As a description of religious experience there is nothing new in this; mystics down the centuries have spoken in these terms. Kierkegaard's originality lay in constructing a coherent philosophy of subjectivity: a kind of theology which was anti-theological.

The foundation of this relationship, according to Kierkegaard, is choice. He says that most people avoid choice by living 'aesthetically', which broadly means relying on instinct and feelings. He does not oppose the aesthetic approach, but says it must be complemented by the 'ethical'. Yet this does not mean choosing between good and evil; nor does it mean choosing whether to believe or not to believe in God. Put simply, it means choosing to choose – recognising that there is a choice to be made. And once this recognition occurs, the outcome must be to choose the good.

This conclusion is both philosophically and morally shocking. Philosophically Kierkegaard transcends the conundrum of freedom and determinism by saying that freedom lies not in choice itself, but at one stage removed: in the freedom to choose whether to choose. And once people have chosen to choose, the outcome is pre-determined: they will see that the only worthwhile choice is to submit to God and his moral laws. Thus Kierkegaard simultaneously upholds freedom and yet accepts determinism. At first sight this seems like sophistry, a clever piece of philosophising that amounts to very little. But it is a remarkably profound description of the actual experience of freedom. Most of us drift through life trying to avoid making real choices and decisions, but relying on a combination of circumstances and feelings to determine our activities. Yet at some point a situation may arise, or our mental state may reach a condition, in which we are impelled to confront what Kierkegaard calls the 'either/or' – a distinction between good and evil. And at the moment of choice, we sense that we have no choice: we must choose that which seems good.

The moral implication is that evil is never, in a strict sense, deliberate. People act in an evil manner, but this is because they are living 'aesthetically', and their emotions and instincts lead them into evil ways. But, in Kierkegaard's understanding, it is impossible to make a clear and free choice in favour of evil. This may seem to exempt people from responsibility for their conduct, and hence from blame and punishment. But in fact Kierkegaard believes that individuals are responsible for whether they live aesthetically or ethically; and he is extremely critical, even judgmental, of those who live purely aesthetically.

In a provocative passage Kierkegaard suggests that boredom is the root of all evil. He contrasts boredom with idleness. Most people, he says, believe that idleness is the root of evil, since idle people become bored, and make mischief to assuage their boredom. But boredom for Kierkegaard is the failure to confront the ethical dilemma at the heart of human existence – and hence the failure truly to live. And paradoxically idleness, properly understood and used, is the means of overcoming boredom. Those who are constantly working hard for material success have neither the time nor inclination to consider ethical matters; and by this thoughtlessness often act in an evil and destructive manner. Idle people, on the other hand, have the opportunity to think deeply, and hence are more likely to live ethically.

The period in which Kierkegaard lived saw great economic progress, based on the triumph of the market mechanism. Kierkegaard regards the freedom of the market-place as illusory, presenting individuals merely with a wider range of goods to stimulate their aesthetic appetites. But he also sees great dangers in the exaltation of this kind of freedom. It gives people the impression that freedom consists in the breaking down of obstacles and constraints, so that individuals can choose what they want. But to Kierkegaard true freedom consists in overcoming constraints, because this involves choice and effort. Through exercising choice, and enacting what they have chosen, people grow in spiritual stature.

The ultimate consequence of failing to choose is despair; and Kierkegaard's analysis of despair is the most moving and poignant of his works. He calls despair 'the sickness unto death'. A bodily sickness may lead to physical death; but in the Christian understanding physical death is a transition into life. Despair, by contrast, is a spiritual sickness, a sickness of the 'self'. And while those suffering despair want to die, their torment lies in their continuing life; despair is a living death. A person may be thrown into despair by a particular event, such as the breaking of a relationship or the failure of an ambition. But the real object of despair is oneself: the person in despair wants to get rid of the self, yet knows that this is impossible. Despair is thus a spiritual paralysis, which is the antithesis of true freedom.

Kierkegaard yearned for saints and heroes who would embody his ideal self, and lamented his failure to find any. But he did try to imagine a true 'knight of faith'; and his description is astonishing because the person he portrays is so ordinary. The knight of faith looks and lives like a simple clerk, doing a humdrum job in an office, and returning home to a modest flat; and like thousands of other clerks he walks in the woods on Sundays. What marks him out is that he takes delight in every scene, every activity and every person. And even if something does not meet his expectations, he enjoys whatever transpires. Kierkegaard defines this spiritual condition as 'resignation', by which he means a renunciation of all desire to possess and control external objects, and hence joyous acceptance of all that is. By renouncing the temporal and the finite, the individual acquires the eternal and the infinite – which is what Kierkegaard means by faith.

This description of spiritual heroism is taken further in his analysis of love. He contrasts the poets' view of love with the Christian view. Poets frequently speak of loving another person more than yourself; but this kind of love is an emotion which is directed towards a particular person, and which will pass. The Christian command, to love others 'as yourself', seems on the face of it less noble and ambitious. But such love is a permanent spiritual attitude which is directed towards all people; and it implies a merging of the individual self or soul with all souls. Moreover Christian love has a finer practical outcome than the poets' love. To love someone more than yourself is to defer to their wishes, even when this causes them harm. But to love someone 'as yourself' is to assess the other person's wishes, as if they were your own; and perhaps refuse to grant them, in order to protect the person from harm.

Kierkegaard has often been described as the first 'existentialist' philosopher, a term as vague as it is ubiquitous. Yet it does point to the heart of his philosophy, and why he continues to attract so many readers. He doggedly avoided all kinds of metaphysical speculation, and thence all kinds of theology, as the subject is normally understood. At the same time he refused to reduce life to any kind of materialist formula, as many of his contemporaries were doing. His purpose was to analyse human existence as people actually experience it, as this meant affirming its dilemmas, its complexities, and its spiritual dimension.

His Life

Søren Aabye was born in Copenhagen on 5 May 1813. He was the seventh child of Michael Pederson

Kierkegaard, whose own family had been serfs working on the land. Michael in his youth had obtained his freedom, and moved to the capital city where he set up a successful hosiery business. His first wife died young, and he married her maid, an illiterate woman whom he soon came to despise – but who bore his large family.

Michael was not only a shrewd businessman, but also a devout Lutheran with a morbid temperament. Far from regarding his worldly achievements as a sign of divine blessing, he was racked by guilt, and lived in constant fear of divine retribution.

This in turn made him cruelly strict towards his children, from whom he demanded total obedience, under threat of the severest punishments. Søren later recalled the religious gloom which pervaded the entire house, and the sense that the whole family was under an unspecified curse. In his *Journal* he wrote of the 'dread with which my father filled my soul, his own frightful melancholy, and all the things in this connection which I cannot even note down'; and he described his upbringing as 'insane'. Nonetheless Søren admired his father's intellectual and imaginative powers: and to an extent his writings can be seen as a prolonged attempt to grapple with his father's legacy.

The unhappiness of Søren's childhood was matched by the misery of his career at school. He was weak and clumsy, and by his own account physically unattractive. So he avoided all sports, and was prey to bullies. He gradually learnt to protect himself with a sharp and sarcastic tongue, which occasionally reduced his antagonists to tears. He was thus a lonely, forlorn figure, regarded by his contemporaries with a mixture of fear and contempt.

At the age of seventeen he enrolled at Copenhagen University. His first year, in which he studied a wide range of subjects, was outstandingly successful. He then decided to specialise in theology, with the intention of becoming a Lutheran pastor. But it evoked so many questions of deep personal concern, that he was unable to follow the prescribed course, and instead read whatever books grasped his attention. He also began to react against the austerities of his upbringing, running up debts for drink and clothes which his father was forced to settle. By his early twenties he had self-consciously adopted the manners and habits of an intellectual socialite, spending the daylight hours in cafés debating politics and philosophy, and going to the theatre or the opera at nights – with, in his own words, 'glasses on his nose and a cigar in his mouth'.

Even at the time he recognised that this way of life was largely a sham; 'with the one face I laugh, with the other I weep', he wrote in his *Journal*. He complained that the pleasures he pursued invariably left him feeling empty and listless, and he yearned for a 'life-view' which could inspire his enthusiasm and give him a sense of purpose. The mask of gaiety was finally broken by the sudden death of his father in 1838. Already five of the seven children had died, and Søren had expected his father to outlive himself and his surviving brother as well. He interpreted his father's death as some kind of 'sacrifice' which had been made on his behalf, so that 'I might turn into something.' The substantial sum he inherited from his father removed from him permanently any need to earn money. Yet he now felt himself under an obligation to his father to complete his studies, and devote himself to a professional career. In 1840, ten years after starting, he was awarded his degree; and in the same year he became engaged to Regine Olsen, the daughter of a senior civil servant. He then embarked on a training course at a pastoral seminary.

But this new respectability proved as much a burden as his earlier decadent style of life. He regretted his proposal of marriage the day after he had made it, but dithered in a state of mounting anxiety for almost a year until returning the ring. Regine tried to win him back; he responded with an air of careless indifference in the hope that he would 'push her into marrying someone else'. The prospect of becoming a pastor now filled him with a sense of moral and spiritual inadequacy, and he became profoundly depressed. So he withdrew from the seminary, and decided to devote himself exclusively to writing. 'To produce,' he remarked later, 'was to be my life.'

In common with many writers, Kierkegaard found that mental anguish, far from detracting from literary endeavour, was a spur. Even during the unhappy period of his engagement, he completed a master's dissertation on the concept of irony in the philosophy of Socrates. His convoluted style, and frequent references to his own inner experiences worried the examiners, but they eventually passed his work. In 1841 he went to Berlin to hear a course of lectures being given by the German philosopher Schelling. At first Kierkegaard was impressed, but then became exasperated by the 'impotence' of Schelling's metaphysical speculation. Indeed, listening to Schelling crystallised in him an aversion to all kinds of theological discourse, and thence a conviction that religious and philosophical ideas should be rooted in the 'subjective'. He returned to Copenhagen, and over the next four years, in an astonishing burst of creativity, he produced seven major books of philosophy, plus eighteen shorter religious works. He described himself as labouring 'like a clerk in his office, with hardly a single day's break'. By 1845 he was mentally exhausted and retired to the country.

Although he published under a variety of pseudonyms, in the relatively small circle of Copenhagen society his authorship was widely known. Most people were perplexed by his ideas, and by the dense prose in which he expressed them; but he gained the reputation for having a highly unorthodox attitude to Christianity. In December 1845 an acquaintance of Kierkegaard's from his student days, P. L. Møller, published an essay attacking Kierkegaard, both for his religious ideas and for his treatment of Regine Olsen. Møller seemingly hoped that this attack would advance his own prospects of being a university professor. Kierkegaard at once returned to Copenhagen, where he wrote a stinging reply. In it he disclosed that Møller covertly contributed to a satirical magazine, *The Corsair*, which held prominent people up to ridicule; he also challenged *The Corsair* to make him one of its victims.

For both Møller and Kierkegaard, their intemperate polemics rebounded on them. Møller's reputation and career were badly damaged by the revelation of his scurrilous activities. Kierkegaard became the object of sustained attack in the column of *The Corsair*, in which his appearance, mannerisms and personal habits, as well as his writings, were cruelly mocked. In his *Journal* he recorded: 'Even the butcher's boy almost thinks himself justified in being offensive to me at the behest of *The Corsair*. Undergraduates grin and giggle, and are delighted that someone prominent should be trodden

down.... The best things I do, such as paying someone a visit, are distorted and misinterpreted, and
repeated everywhere.' He even found that his friends
were avoiding him, for fear that they too might
become victims by association. 'In the end,'
Kierkegaard concluded, 'the only thing will be to
withdraw, and go about with those I dislike, because
I merely bring shame on those I like.'

Kierkegaard never fully recovered from the
trauma of this episode. Having attempted to become
part of Copenhagen society, he reverted to the iso-
lation of his earlier years, distrusting all but his clos-
est companions; and an element of bitterness entered
his writings. Yet this episode also helped to renew
and deepen his Christian faith. Having seen how
readily people accept untruths, he felt he had a particular vocation to speak out for the truth – and that
he had the intellectual and literary gifts for this task.
He was called to 'steer into the open sea, depending
entirely on the grace of God'. During the following
five years he wrote six major religious books, each
of which was an extraordinary combination of philosophy, mysticism, Biblical exegesis and psychology.
In them he probed every aspect of religious experience, from the nature of Christian love, to the spiritual death which comes from despair. These books
contain an emotional passion that was missing from
his earlier works, as he tries to stand alone before

God, discerning God's message for the present age.

But if Kierkegaard emerges as a prophet in his religious works, he did not adopt the austerities traditionally associated with this role. On the contrary, he drew heavily on his inheritance to furnish his apartment in the most elegant style, to hire carriages to take him for drives in the country, and to indulge his taste for good food and fine wine – elaborate meals were daily brought to him from the best restaurants. He was a little ashamed of his extravagance, particularly as in his books he was condemning contemporary society for its hypocrisy and complacency. But he publicly justified it as the necessary context for his genius to flourish.

During the early 1850s Kierkegaard published very little. But in 1854 an incident in the Church triggered his last major work. The Danish primate died, and was replaced by Hans Martensen, who had been one of Kierkegaard's tutors at university. Kierkegaard had never liked Martensen, and had come to regard him as exemplifying the self-satisfied and complacent approach to Christianity which he abhorred. Thus in December of that year he wrote a long article attacking Martensen in particular, and official Christianity in general – which he called 'Christendom'. He argued that the Church had become essentially a secular institution, operating in partnership with the State; and it was ruled by a bureaucracy whose main aim was to further its own material interest. As a result, the Church had become a living contradiction of the gospel which Christ preached. Having published the article, Kierkegaard felt compelled to withdraw altogether from formal worship. He became once again the object of vicious attack – this time from the ecclesiastical and political establishment; and there was even talk of official legal action against him.

He was probably aware that his health was now failing. In the spring of 1855 he wrote for his own edification a short and intensely moving essay on the relationship of human beings to God. In it he explores the apparent passivity of God, who allows himself to be mocked or ignored without retaliating. Kierkegaard interprets this as a sign of both the 'unchangeableness' of God, and also his patience. He concludes that, when other people come to appreciate God's immutability, they find peace and security within it; through their relationship with God, they feel they are 'coming home'. It was a fitting final testament. Early in October of that year, he collapsed in the street, and died in hospital a few weeks later. It was a measure of the grudging respect which people had for his genius that his funeral was held at Copenhagen Cathedral. And in the address his elder brother, who was a respectable Lutheran pastor, spoke for the assembled congregation in both praising

Søren's intelligence, and regretting his lack of sound judgment.

* * *

Kierkegaard wrote exclusively in his native language, so during his life-time he was completely unknown outside Denmark. Some of his books were translated into German after his death, but made little impact. It was not until the following century, in the period after the First World War, that he began to be acknowledged as a modern prophet. This was just as Kierkegaard himself had predicted: in his *Journal* he said that it would take many decades for people to grasp the importance of his message.

He is now fêted as one of the great philosophers of the nineteenth century, and Copenhagen has proudly created a statue in his honour. Professors give lectures on his thought, and undergraduates grapple with his prose. Yet Kierkegaard consistently denounced this intellectual and 'objective' approach to truth, and denounced too the professors who promoted it. His consistent theme, that the source of truth is subjective experience, leaves little room for academic philosophy. He is perhaps better described as a mystic – a mystic who, recognising the paradox in such a venture, tried to develop a philosophy of mysticism.

While his books sell better now than ever before, it is doubtful how much more widely he is read;

many purchasers attempt a few paragraphs, and give up in frustration at his style. The present selection is an attempt to remedy this. It contains extracts from most of his major works, and covers all his main ideas. Every attempt has been to render his prose into readable English, while remaining faithful to the original. The pieces are presented in chronological order.

ROBERT VAN DE WEYER

OVERCOMING BOREDOM

---

from *Either/Or* (1843)

I will start from a principle affirmed by experience: all people are bores.... Surely no one will prove to be so great a bore as to contradict me in this. This principle is in the very highest degree repellent, which is an essential quality of all negative principles – and negative principles are in truth the basis of all motion. It is not merely repellent, but also intensely forbidding; and for these reasons it has great power to push people forward, helping them to make new discoveries. If my principle is true, it puts humanity in a desperate plight; and when people realise just how bored they are, they spring into activity to try and relieve their boredom. And if one wants to attain the maximum degree of activity, almost to the point of endangering the driving-power of that activity, one need only say to oneself: 'Boredom is the root of all evil.' It is strange that boredom, itself so stable and unmoving, should possess such power to stimulate activity. One might almost think its power is magical – except that its power comes not from attraction, but from repulsion.

In the case of children, the terrible effects of

boredom are recognised by everyone. Children behave well so long as they are enjoying themselves. This is true in the strictest sense. If they start to behave badly when they seem to be enjoying themselves, it is because they are beginning to be bored – boredom is already approaching, perhaps unexpectedly. Thus a good teacher should not only be upright, hard-working and competent, but should also have the imagination to keep children amused....

Since boredom is the root of all evil, the world goes from bad to worse; and its evils multiply, as boredom increases. Indeed, the history of the world from the very beginning is the history of boredom. The gods were bored, so they created man. Adam was bored on his own, so Eve was created. So boredom entered the world; and as the population increased, so did boredom. Adam was bored alone; Adam and Eve were bored together; Adam, Eve, Cain and Abel were bored as a family; and as the population rose, entire peoples and nations were bored.

It is often said that idleness is the root of all evil. And to prevent this evil people are urged to work. But it is easy to see, both from that nature of the evil itself and from the remedy proposed, that this attitude is extremely crude. Idleness cannot possibly be the root of evil; on the contrary, idleness is truly divine – provided one is not bored. Idleness may cause people to lose their wealth; but those who are high-minded are indifferent to such dangers – they fear only boredom. The Olympian gods were not bored; they lived happily in their idleness. A beautiful woman, who does not sew, spin, bake, read or play the piano, is happy in her idleness, since she is not bored. Far from being the root of evil, idleness is the only true good.

Boredom is the root of all evil, and so it must be kept at a distance. Idleness is not an evil. Those who lack a sense of idleness prove that their minds are at a very low level of development. They suffer from a restlessness, a constant need for activity, which excludes them from the world of the spirit; they are like animals, whose instincts impel them constantly to be on the move. They are the kind of people who turn everything into a matter of business; they fall in love, marry, listen to a joke, or admire a work of art with the same industrious zeal they apply to their work. The Latin proverb, 'Idleness is the devil's pillow,' contains a measure of truth; but the devil cannot reach the pillow of someone who is not bored….

Since, as I have shown, boredom is the root of all evil, what can be more natural than the effort to assuage it? As in all matters, we must think calmly about this; otherwise the devilish spirit of boredom might drive us deeper and deeper into the mire, even as we try to escape. Everyone who feels bored cries out for a change. I feel entirely in sympathy with this. But one must act according to a stable principle.

I differ from the ordinary view as to how boredom may be assuaged. My principle may be expressed in the word 'rotation'. This word has a degree of ambiguity. It could suggest constantly moving around from place to place. But the farmer does not use it in this sense.

Let us consider rotation for a moment in its first sense: that of constant physical movement. This is very vulgar, and depends on an illusion. People tire of living in the country, so they move to the city; they tire of their native land, so they travel abroad; they tire of Europe, so they go to America; finally all they can do is dream of endless journeys from star to star. Or there is another kind of physical movement, which in reality is the same: people tire of porcelain dishes, so they eat off silver; they tire of silver, and turn to gold. In the same way an emperor burns half of Rome to get an idea of burning Troy. This kind of movement is self-defeating; it is as endless as stillness. What did Nero gain by his action?

My method does not consist in a change of field; rather it resembles agricultural rotation, in which the crop and mode of cultivation are changed. This leads to the principle of limitation, the only principle which can save the world. The more you limit yourself, the more fertile and creative you become. A prisoner in solitary confinement may become highly creative; he can create his own entertainment in watching a spider. Think back to your schooldays, when many of your teachers were dull and tiresome: how fertile you were in finding things to engage your interest! The more restricted the circumstances, the more closely you observe even the tiniest noise or movement. Boredom is overcome through becoming intensive in your interests, not extensive.

The more resourceful you can be in changing the mode of cultivation, the better. But every particular change will involve both remembering and forgetting. Life as a whole moves according to these two currents, so it is essential to have them under control.... No moment should be regarded as so significant that it cannot be forgotten at your convenience. Equally each moment should have such significance that it can be remembered at will. Childhood, which is the period of life you remember best, is also the period of which you have forgotten most. The more poetically you remember, the easier you forget; for remembering poetically is really only another expression for forgetting. In poetic memory experiences undergo transformation, by which they lose all their painful aspects. To remember in this way, you must be careful how you live, and also how you enjoy yourself. Enjoying experiences to their full intensity for their full duration makes it impossible either to remember or to forget them. You remember the sense of being overwhelmed; you would prefer to forget this, but it constantly comes back against your will to plague you. So when you begin to notice that a certain pleasure or experience is gaining too strong a hold on your mind, you should pause and reflect. This will make you want to stop the experience. From the start you should keep every enjoyment under control, never giving yourself totally to it. You should embark on each pleasurable experience with caution and even wariness....

When you have perfected in yourself the twin arts of remembering and forgetting you are in a position to play badminton with the whole of life, hitting the shuttlecock to and fro.

PASSION, PLEASURE AND PAIN

from *Either/Or* (1843)

Other people may complain that the present age is wicked. I complain that it is wretched, because it lacks passion. People's souls are thin and flimsy like lace; and they themselves are mere spiritual lacemakers. The thoughts of their hearts are too paltry to be regarded as sinful. A worm might be looked upon as sinful to think in such a way; but for people made in the image of God, 'sinful' is too big a word. Their desires are drab and sluggish, their passion lethargic. They are like shopkeepers, doing their duty, but clipping little pieces of gold from the coins they take. They think that, even if the Lord is careful in keeping his accounts, they can cheat him a little. Away with them! This is why my soul constantly turns back to the Old Testament and to Shakespeare. The characters there are real human beings: they hate and love, they murder their enemies, they curse their descendants, they sin.

* * *

The essence of pleasure does not lie in the thing enjoyed, but in the consciousness which accompanies it. Imagine that I have a servant who is eager to please. I ask him for a glass of water, but instead he brings me a chalice containing a blend of the finest wines. I will dismiss him, in order to teach him that pleasure consists not in what I enjoy, but in having my own way.

* * *

Wine no longer makes my heart glad; a little wine makes me sad, and a lot makes me melancholy. My soul is faint and impotent. I prick the flank of my soul with the spur of pleasure, but there is no reaction; my soul does not leap. I have lost my illusions. I try in vain to plunge into the great ocean of enjoyment; but it will not receive me – or, rather, I cannot stand it. There was once a time when, if pleasure beckoned, I ran towards it, swift and light of foot, without fear. In the past, when I rode through the woods, I seemed to fly; now my horse is as creaky and weary as I am, and we barely seem to move. I now prefer my own company. It is not that others have deserted me; that would not hurt me. Rather I have been deserted by the happy fairies of joy, who used to throng around me, guiding me towards witty and hedonistic friends. Just as a drunkard gathers a wild crowd of youths around him, so these fairies of joy flocked around me; and I welcomed them with a smile. If I had a single wish, I would not wish for wealth and power. No, I would wish for passion, for a sense of the possible pleasure in each situation – for a young and ardent eye which sees potential happiness all around. Pleasure itself may disappoint, but possibility never does. And what wine is so full, so fragrant, so intoxicating as possibility?

* * *

Music can reach places which the rays of the sun do not penetrate. My room is dark and dismal; a high wall outside the window almost excludes the light of day. Yet I hear a sound from a neighbouring yard. Perhaps it is made by a wandering musician. What instrument is he playing? Is it a flute? What do I hear? The minuet from *Don Juan*! Carry me away, you rich and powerful tones, to the company of beautiful girls, to the pleasure of dancing. I can hear the apothecary pounding his mortar, the kitchen maid scouring the kettle, the groom combing the horse and striking his instrument against the flag-stones. But the sound of the music is for me alone; they are beckoning only me. Accept my gratitude, whoever you are. You have enriched and strengthened my soul. For these few moments you have poured the wine of joy into my soul.

* * *

My sadness is my castle. It is an eagle's nest built high up in the mountain peaks above the clouds. Nothing can storm it. From it I fly down into reality to seize my prey. But I do not remain down there; I bring my prey home, and I weave it into a sombre tapestry. I live as one who has died. I immerse everything I have experienced into the baptismal waters of forgetfulness. I think only of the eternal; everything finite and temporal is erased from the memory.

* * *

The sun shines into my room; it is bright and beautiful. The window is open in the next room. Outside the window the street is quiet; it is Sunday afternoon. In the garden of a neighbour's house, where a pretty young lady lives, I can hear a lark sing with great energy. Far away in a distant street I hear a vendor shouting 'Shrimps.' The air is so warm, yet the whole town seems dead. Then I think of my youth and of my first love. I recall the strength of my desire, of my longing. Now my only desire is for such desire to return. What is youth? A dream. What is love? The substance of a dream.

* * *

Something wonderful has happened to me. I was carried up into the seventh heaven. There all the gods had assembled, and were seated in front of me. By divine grace I was allowed to make a wish. 'Will you,' asked Mercury, 'have youth, or beauty, or power, or a long life, or the most beautiful wife, or any of the other wonderful blessings we have in this chest? Choose; but you can choose only one.' For a moment I was at a loss. Then I spoke to the gods: 'Most honourable beings, I choose that I may always have laughter on my side.' Not one of the gods said a word, but they all began to laugh. I concluded that my request was granted. The gods knew how to express themselves appropriately; it would hardly have been right to have answered in solemn tones, 'Your wish is granted.'

CHOOSING TO CHOOSE

———————◆———————

from *Either/Or* (1843)

I have said often in the past, and I say again now, or rather I shout it: 'either/or'. There are situations where it would be stupid or mad to apply an either/or. Equally there are people whose souls are too feeble to grasp what is implied in such a challenge, and who thus lack the energy to cry out either/or. These words have always made a deep impression on me. And they still do, especially when I express them with conviction and without reference to any specific issue. Using them suggests the possibility of making clear choices between different courses of action. They affect me like some magical incantation; and my soul becomes very solemn, even anguished.

I think of my early years, when I did not know fully how to make choices. I listened to the instructions of my elders with childish trust. At times I felt I was making solemn choices, but in reality I was doing what I had been taught. I think of occasions in adulthood, when I have stood at the crossroads, with my soul struggling to make a decision. I think of other occasions, less momentous but still important, when I have had to turn this way or that. There is only one type of situation in which either/or has absolute significance: when truth, justice and holiness are lined up on one side, and lust, warped inclinations and dark passions are lined up on the other. Yet in every situation it is good to make a careful choice, even when both alternatives are morally acceptable....

The phrase 'either/or' is frequently on your lips; indeed you rarely stop using it. Yet what significance has it for you? None at all. As far as I can tell, it is a kind of gesture, like the wink of an eye, or the wave of a hand – an abracadabra. You know how to slip it into different situations, to have maximum effect. It also has a great effect on you, intoxicating you as alcohol intoxicates a person with mental illness. You refer to this intoxication as 'higher madness'. You claim that 'either/or' is the essence of practical wisdom. And you illustrate this with the story about that great thinker and philosopher who was once insulted by another man. The philosopher responded by pulling off the man's hat, throwing it to the floor, and exclaiming: 'If you pick it up, I'll thrash you; if you do not pick it up, I'll also thrash you. You can choose....'

You take great delight in comforting people when they come to you in difficult situations. You listen to them describing their predicament, and then say: 'Yes,

I see clearly there are two possibilities. You can either do this or do that. My sincere opinion and friendly advice is to do this and to do that – you will regret both.' But those who mock others also mock themselves. Your response is not merely empty, but is a profound mockery of yourself: a sorry proof of how limp your soul is....

You excuse yourself by saying that life is a masquerade, and thus an inexhaustible source of amusement. As a result of your attitude, no one has succeeded in getting to know you. Every revelation you make about yourself is an illusion. Only in this way are you able to breathe; you push people away from you, to give yourself space to survive. You devote yourself to protecting your hiding-place; you strive to retain an enigmatic mask over yourself. But in truth you are nothing. You exist merely in relation to other people; and you are what you are by virtue of that relation....

You can see from what I am saying how different my view of choice is from yours – if you can truly be said to have a view. Indeed, your view differs from mine in the fact that it prevents real choice. For me the moment of choice is immensely serious. This is not because I necessarily make great efforts to weigh the alternatives. Nor is it because I look carefully at the potential consequences. Rather it is because I sense danger afoot: danger that the moment of choice will quickly pass, and that I will find myself merely repeating past experiences. It is an illusion to think that, even for an instant, you can make your personality neutral; or that you can break the course of your life and bring it to a halt. Your personality is involved with the choice before it is made. Equally, if you postpone making a choice, it is because your personality has unconsciously interfered. And sometimes choices are made not by deliberate thought, but by deep forces within the personality.

When at last a choice is made, you often discover that you must go back over something you have done in the past; you must revoke past mistakes. This is very difficult. We read in fairy tales about human beings who heard the demonic music of mermaids and mermen, and were enticed into their power. According to these stories the only way a person can break the spell is to play the same music backwards, without making a single mistake. Equally in life the only way to eradicate the errors of the past is to go backwards over the past event, and not to make the errors again.

This is why it is important to make choices – and to make them at the right time....

What, then, is the essence of my either/or? Is it a choice between good and evil? Not exactly. I want only to bring you to the point where the choice between good and evil has some significance for you.

Everything hinges on this for you. As soon as one can get a person to stand at a crossroads, where a choice must be made, the person will choose what is right. Thus if, while you are reading this lengthy dissertation, you happen to find yourself in a position of facing a choice, then throw the rest of my dissertation away – do not concern yourself with it any more. Just choose. You will then experience for yourself the value of making a choice. Let me assure you that a young girl always prefers to choose a man who knows how to choose.

So, then, a person either has to live aesthetically, or has to live ethically. In this alternative there is not in the strict sense any question of choice. The person who lives aesthetically, responding only to feelings and emotions, does not choose. And the person who, having considered the ethical way of life, chooses the aesthetical, is not living aesthetically; that person's way of life has resulted from an ethical choice, even though it may be described as unethical. There is an indelible imprint on an ethical way of life; even though it may be barely superior to an aesthetical way of life, it is the product of choice.

This unethical way of life, based on a rejection of ethics, is a quiet form of hell. People who adopt it do not truly live. The events of their lives may unfold one after the other. But as individuals they vanish like shadows; they are not really participating in their

own existence; their immortal souls are blown away
– and yet they are not worried about the problem of
immortality, because they are already spiritually dead.
They do not live aesthetically, but neither are they
living fully in an ethical manner; they have neither
embraced nor rejected the ethical way of life. They
are not sinning, except insofar as it is sinful to choose
not to choose. Nor do they doubt their immortality;
those who deeply and honestly doubt their immortality are truly alive.

My either/or does not in the first instance denote
the choice between good and evil. It denotes the
choice as to whether one will choose between good
and evil, or whether one will not choose. In reality
the question is, whether having contemplated one's
existence as a whole, once chooses to live. Those who
choose to live thereby also choose to be faced with a
continual choice between good and evil – although
this may only become apparent afterwards. To live
aesthetically is not evil, but neutral; this is why I
affirmed that choice is intrinsically ethical. It is, therefore, not so much a choice between having a good
will and an evil will; it is a choice actually to have a
will. Only then does one confront the choice
between good and evil....

Thus you see how important it is to make a
choice. The crucial thing is not deliberation, but the
baptism of the will – the recognition that ethical

choices have to be made. The longer this baptism is delayed, the more difficult it becomes; the soul becomes more and more attached to the aesthetical way of life, and so it becomes harder to tear it loose. Yet this is necessary if one is truly to choose.

FAITH AND RESIGNATION

———◆———

from *Fear and Trembling* (1843)

Would it be better if people no longer questioned their faith and instead concentrated on standing upright within their faith? The paradox of faith is that it has numerous absurdities; yet those who are moved by it gain great benefits, even in this world. For my part I can describe these movements of faith which bring such blessings, but I cannot make them....

I have searched for people whom one could describe as 'knights of faith'; but I have found no one who convincingly fits that description. Perhaps I am missing them; perhaps every second person is a knight of faith. Yet I have been looking for several years, and my efforts have been in vain. People commonly travel across the world to see rivers and mountains, new stars, birds with unusual plumage, oddly shaped fish, even other races who look different from their own. They gape with foolish wonder at these strange sights, and think they have learnt something important. None of this interests me. But I would be profoundly interested to hear about a knight of faith; and I would make a pilgrimage on foot to meet that person. I would fix my ears and eyes on him, trying to observe how faith moves him. At last I would feel secure; I would divide the rest of my life between watching him and imitating him – thus I would spend all my time admiring him.

As I have said, I have not met such a person, but I can easily imagine him. Here he is. Having reached him, I am introduced to him. The moment I set eyes on him, I push him away from me. I myself leap backwards, clasping my hands, and exclaim in a shocked whisper: 'Good Lord, is this the man? Is this really the person? Why, he looks like a tax collector!' But it is indeed the man. I draw closer to him, watching even his smallest movements to see if there is some sign – like a short telegraphic message – of his communion with the infinite; to see if some glance, expression, gesture, note of melancholy, or smile might indicate that in him the infinite touches the finite. No! I examine his figure from top to toe to look for a cranny through which the infinite might be peeping. No! He is solid from top to bottom. His gait? It is vigorous, belonging entirely to the finite; no smartly dressed citizen going for a walk to Fresburg on a Sunday afternoon treads the ground more firmly. He belongs entirely to the world; no Philistine is more rooted in the world than he is. One can find nothing of that aloof and superior manner one might expect in a knight of the infinite.

He takes delight in everything. Whenever he takes part in some particular activity, he does it with the persistence which is the mark of an earthly man; his soul is manifestly absorbed in the activity. He is so precise that, looking at him, one might imagine that he is a clerk who has given his soul to an intricate system of book-keeping. He observes Sunday as a holiday. He goes to church. Nothing about him indicates any special spiritual qualities. If one did not know otherwise, it would be impossible to distinguish him from the rest of the congregation. His lusty and vigorous hymn-singing tells us that he has a strong chest – that is all. In the afternoon he walks to the forest. He takes delight in everything he sees: the crowds of people; the new vehicles on the street; the sound of water. If one were to meet him on the road to the beach, one might suppose he was a shopkeeper taking a fling. I look in vain for some sign of a poetic imagination, but I can find none, because in truth he is not a poet.

As evening approaches he walks home, with the tireless stride of a postman. On his way home he happily speculates on the special warm dish that his wife has prepared for him; perhaps, he wonders, it will be roasted calf's head, garnished with vegetables. If he were to meet a man similar to himself also going home, he would walk with him as far as the East Gate, discussing the food they were about to enjoy with the passion of a hotel chef. In fact he has not even four pence to his name, but he firmly believes that his wife will have prepared a beautiful meal. If she had cooked such a meal, it would be an invidious sight for superior people, and an inspiring one for plain men, to watch him eat, for his appetite is greater than Esau's. But his wife has not prepared anything special; and, strangely enough, he does not mind....

He sits by an open window of his apartment, and looks down on the square below. He is interested in everything that goes on: in a rat which slips under the kerb; in the children playing; in the teenage girls hanging about. But he is no genius; in vain I have looked for signs of genius. In the evening he smokes a pipe. Watching him one would swear that he was the local grocer relaxing in the twilight. He seems utterly care-free, yet he always uses his time productively.

In all this he lives simultaneously in the infinite and the finite; in everything he does, he is making the movements of infinity. I am furious with him, for no other reason than I am envious. He has shown infinite resignation, infinite acceptance of life as it is; and in this way he has drained the profound sadness from life. He knows the bliss of the infinite. He senses the pain of renouncing everything, even the dearest things he possesses in the world; yet he knows through renunciation life in this world is hugely enhanced. To him the simple, common things of life are as good as the most exotic. He is simultaneously very normal, and also a new creation. He has renounced everything, and also possesses everything. He constantly makes the movements of infinity, but does so with such precision and assurance that he lives fully in the finite.

Faith, therefore, is not an aesthetic emotion, but something far higher. It is based on resignation, on renunciation. It is not an immediate instinct of the heart, but is a paradox at the heart of life.... The act of resignation is the foundation of faith, but does not require faith. Through resignation I gain an awareness of eternity; this is a philosophical change in my attitude, which I can train myself to make. Whenever I feel overwhelmed by finite concerns, I deliberately draw back from them and turn my mind and heart towards God, who is eternal and infinite. As I say, faith is not required for the act of resignation, but it is needed for going beyond an awareness of eternity. And this is where things become paradoxical. Resignation and faith are frequently confused, because it is said that people need faith to renounce their claim to worldly things. Indeed one hears a stranger thing than this. People lament their loss of faith; but when one looks closely at them, one sees that they never had faith, but had merely made an act of resignation.

In the act of resignation I renounce everything. This is a movement I make by my own effort. If I fail to make it, this is because I am cowardly, weak-minded and apathetic, and thus do not feel the great responsibility which has been given to all human beings to be their own censors – a far greater responsibility than that of being Censor General to the whole Roman Republic. Having made this movement myself, I gain awareness of eternity, and thus enter a loving relationship with the Eternal Being, whom we call God.

Faith is not about renunciation. On the contrary, through faith I acquire everything – precisely in the sense that, according to Christ's teaching, faith even as small as a mustard seed can move mountains. A purely human courage is required to renounce all temporal things, in order to gain the eternal. Yet in faith I cannot renounce the eternal – that would be a self-contradiction. Thus paradox enters the very notion of faith; and a humble courage is to grasp it – the courage of faith.

SUBJECTIVE AND OBJECTIVE TRUTH

from *Concluding Unscientific Postscript* (1846)

The question at issue is not the truth of Christianity. It is foolish to assume that if its objective truth could be determined, people would be ready and willing to accept it. The key question is the mode of the subjective acceptance. It is an illusion to think that the subjective decision does not really exist – that once the objective truth has been established, there will be a smooth transition to subjective acceptance. This illusion is rooted in a profound ignorance of the nature of subjective decision-making, and is a desire to shirk the anguish of subjective choice.

Christianity purports to bestow on people eternal happiness. This is a gift which cannot be distributed wholesale, but only to one individual at a time. Christianity assumes that in each individual there is the inherent potential of accepting this gift – that subjectively everyone is capable of appropriating it. Yet equally Christianity recognises that individuals may not be ready to accept it; and that many people, without further guidance, lack any real appreciation of its significance. Thus individuals need to develop and be transformed, learning to understand themselves in relation to this gift of eternal happiness, which is the greatest gift infinity can bestow on the finite. In other words, individuals must realise their subjective potential. In this sense Christianity is not concerned with objectivity; it wants individuals to be wholly concerned with themselves. Subjectivity is the concern of Christianity; it is only in subjectivity that truth exists – if it exists at all. Objectively Christianity has no reality. If the truth of Christianity existed subjectively in only one person, Christianity would thereby be true – in that person alone. And there is greater Christian joy in heaven over this one individual than over any number of universal theories and theological systems.

It is commonly assumed that no art or skill is required in order to be objective. This is true in the sense that human beings have continuous subjective experience. But we are talking about individuals striving to become what they already are. Who would take the trouble and the time to undertake such a task, involving the greatest degree of renunciation? Indeed, since it involves renunciation, it is an extremely difficult task – the most difficult of all tasks. Yet every human being has a strong natural inclination and passion to develop and be transformed. On the face of it subjective transformation appears rather insignificant; and this apparent insignificance makes people less inclined to undertake it –

they aspire towards some kind of objective transformation. Individuals must make a great effort to recognise that subjective transformation is their true task – it alone can satisfy their inner aspirations.

When the question of truth is raised in terms of objectivity, the truth is presented as an object to which the knower is related. But people are not invited to reflect on this relationship; instead they are asked to contemplate the truth itself. And in this way the individual is said to participate in the truth. When the question of truth is raised in terms of objectivity, individuals are invited to reflect on their relationship with truth. If the mode of this relationship is truthful, then – and only then – is the individual said to participate in the truth. Truth consists in the relationship not in its object.

As an example, let us consider the knowledge of God. Looked at objectively the question is whether the object of knowledge is truly God. Looked at subjectively the question is whether the individual is truly involved in a divine relationship. On which side is the truth to be found? We could resort to mediation, and say: it is on neither side, but in the mediation of both. That would be satisfactory, provided we can explain how an actual individual can be in a state of mediation. A state of mediation implies some kind of stability; but a subjective divine relationship implies that the individual is constantly changing – is being transformed. Besides, individuals cannot be in two places at the same time; they cannot be both subjective and objective simultaneously. People may be subjectively passionate about something they believe to be objectively true; but passion is momentary, and is the highest expression of subjectivity.

Those who choose to follow the objective way find themselves in a process of continuously trying to improve their knowledge, in the hope that this virtually proves God to exist. But this is an impossible quest, because God is a subject, and therefore exists only in terms of subjective awareness. Those who choose the subjective way see instantly the difficulties of finding God objectively, and recognise the vast amount of time this quest would use. They sympathise deeply with those pursuing the objective way, because they know for themselves how painful it is to be separate from God; every moment without God is a moment lost. The subjective way leads people directly to God. They are not required to engage in any kind of intellectual reflection. Rather they must have an infinite passion for subjective truth.

The objective accent falls on what is said, while the subjective accent falls on how it is said. This distinction holds true in the aesthetic, as well as the religious, realm. It receives clear expression in the principle that a statement may be objectively true, but in the mouth of a particular person becomes untrue.... Objectively, interest is focused on the context of a statement; subjectively, interest is focused on the attitudes and feelings which lie behind it. At its maximum intensity, the subjective 'how' is passion for the infinite; and passion for the infinite is truth. Passion for the infinite is subjective; and this subjectivity becomes truth.

In the objective way there is never a moment of decision. The objective way involves spending great effort in trying to define the difference between good and evil, in eliminating all contradictions, and thus delineating clearly the distinction between truth and falsehood. Only in this subjective way is there a moment of decision – a decision which recognises that the objective way is mistaken. Passion for the infinite is the decisive factor, not the content of the infinite. Subjectivity, and the subjective 'how', constitute the truth.

But, since the subject is an actual individual, the subjective 'how' must unfold through time. In the passionate moment of decision, where the road swings away from objective knowledge, it seems as if the decision is instantly fulfilled. But the individual still exists within the temporal order, and the subjective 'how' becomes a matter of striving. This striving receives its impulse and stimulus from the decisive passion for the infinite; but it is striving nonetheless.

When subjectivity is truth, the definition of truth must make clear that subjectivity is the antithesis of objectivity; it must mark the fork in the road where the two ways diverge. And it must also indicate the tension involved in the subjective way. Here is such a definition of truth: an objective uncertainty which is appropriated within a subjective passion. At the point where the two ways diverge (and this point cannot be specified objectively, since it is a subjective matter), objective truth is placed in abeyance. Objectively the subject is now in a state of uncertainty; and this uncertainty increases the tension which the passion for the infinite induces. The truth is that virtue which is rooted in passion for the infinite, thereby chooses objective uncertainty.

I contemplate nature in the hope of finding God. I see within nature omnipotence and wisdom; but I also see much else which disturbs my mind and causes anxiety. For this reason inwardness – the subjective way – becomes acutely intense; it embraces objective uncertainty with the same passion that it has for the infinite. In the case of a mathematical proposition, the objectivity is irrefutable; but for this reason the truth of such a proposition is of no consequence.

The above definition of truth is also a definition of faith. Without risk there is no faith. Faith is that contradiction between subjective passion for the infinite, and objective uncertainty. If I were capable of grasping God objectively, I would not have faith. It is because I cannot do this that I require faith. If I wish to retain my faith, I must constantly hold fast to the objective uncertainty.

RELIGIOUS SUFFERING

from *Concluding Unscientific Postscript* (1846)

Last Sunday the clergyman said: 'You must not depend on the world, nor on other people, nor on yourself, but only on God; for human beings by themselves can do nothing.' We all understood what he was saying, myself included, for this kind of religious morality is very easy to understand. A child can understand it; the most simple-minded individual can understand it quite clearly. It means that we are powerless, we should renounce everything, forsake everything. But it is very difficult to put into practice. On Sunday it is understood with fearful ease – fearful in that all good resolutions are adopted with similar ease. In the abstract we are happy with it. On Monday by contrast it becomes very difficult to understand, because now we have to apply it to the concrete situations in which we live. The man of power is tempted to forget humility. The humble people are tempted to betray their humility before God, by becoming humble towards their superiors, justifying themselves on the grounds of expedience. And when the following Sunday the clergyman complains that no one is acting according to his admonition, his congregation well understands what he means....

But let us imagine people taking to heart what the clergyman says on Sunday, and deciding to live by it. They infer from the clergyman's words that the distinction between ability and lack of ability is a kind of joke. Does this mean that they will no longer try to achieve anything? Will they conclude that all human effort is vain and useless? No, because that would mean missing the joke. It is only by trying to achieve things that they are reminded of how powerless they are. Their vain efforts constantly remind them that they are creatures of vanity. If they were lazy and inactive, regarding themselves as above normal human toil, they would become proud. But to sleep little and to work hard through every waking hour, and then to acknowledge that the whole thing is a joke – that indicates true spiritual seriousness....

Yet this kind of faith in God, and in his promise of eternal happiness, does gradually affect the actions and attitudes of individuals, transforming every aspect of their daily lives. They become less and less concerned with immediate issues, until they become wholly absorbed by their relationship with God. This relationship is no longer some passing thing, but is present and real at every moment. They live with a constant awareness of the closeness of death; and this checks any enthusiasm for immediate pleasures. They become like birds imprisoned in a cage, who still flit here and there; or like fish lying on dry ground, who still twitch as if they were swimming in deep water. They feel imprisoned; they feel out of their element. They become like sick people who cannot move because of the pain they feel everywhere, and yet who cannot prevent themselves from moving so long as they remain alive. Religious people are confined within the finite, and relationship with God makes that confinement horribly painful. Neither the bird in the cage, nor the fish on the shore, nor the invalid on a sickbed, nor a prisoner in the narrowest cell, is so confined as those who are imprisoned in their relationship with God. Just as God is omnipresent, so that sense of confinement is everywhere and at every moment....

In their suffering religious people know that self-indulgence would bring no relief, and so they must refuse to listen to anyone suggesting such a course. They stand before God, and so must endure the full consequences of being human. They gain no comfort from the conversation of those who do not share their predicament, who have only a seventeenth-hand notion of what it means to stand before God. From God alone they must derive their consolation; if they looked elsewhere, their religion would be exposed as a fraud. They should not seek to discover new truths. They should simply keep watch over themselves, controlling any lingering desire for gossip or for

theological speculation; to satisfy that desire would
undermine their religious experience, which count-
less thousands have had in the past.

DOCTRINE AND DECISION

―――――◆―――――

from *Concluding Unscientific Postscript* (1846)

Objectively becoming or being a Christian is defined as accepting the doctrine of Christianity. But this begs the question: what is this doctrine? And in seeking an answer to this question, your attention is instantly turned outwards. You try to learn, down to the last detail, the various orthodox propositions, in order to determine not merely what Christianity is, but whether you are a Christian. You begin the erudite, anxious, fearful and contradictory process of pinning down religion. This process can be protracted indefinitely, so that the decision about your own religious position is relegated to oblivion.

People have tried to resolve this dilemma by claiming that everyone in Christendom is a Christian, that all of us are somehow believers. This notion seems to improve matters for the objective concept of Christianity. Theologians studying the Bible investigate objectively what Christianity is, in order to tell us what we already are; and they assume this objective information will affirm our religion, in the sense that we will come to know the religion that we already believe. Indeed, if we were not already

Christian, this kind of objective theology would not make us Christian. Having been told in an objective fashion what our religion really is, we are then – so it is assumed – able to defend ourselves against the Turk and the Russian and the Roman yoke. And we are expected to fight gallantly for Christianity, in order that our present age might become, as it were, a bridge to a wonderful future which we glimpsed.

But all this is aesthetic nonsense. Christianity must be communicated, not merely affirmed. The task we face is to become Christian and to sustain our faith. The idea that we must be able to defend Christendom against the Turk is the most dangerous of all illusions. On the contrary, our faith should shatter our illusions about the Turk....

Subjectively becoming a Christian is about making a personal decision. The adoption of the Christian faith involves a strange spiritual process which is quite different from any other. Being a Christian is not defined by what Christianity is, but by how a person exists as a Christian. This points to an absolute paradox. There should be no vague talk to the effect that being a Christian is to accept certain articles of belief – all of which are anyway purely rhetorical and fictitious. To believe is a spiritual, not an intellectual, thing. Faith starts from a recognition that we are uncertain about objective truth, and forms an antagonism towards the absurdity of pretending otherwise. From this starting-point, faith becomes a spiritual passion for the infinite, a passion that wants to go beyond objectivity. This passion is quite distinct from the passion of a lover, an enthusiast, or a scientist, because it does not have an object.

The paradox of faith is this. If it were possible for us to gain some higher degree of knowledge so that we could perceive the infinite directly, then we would cease to have faith. Yet faith can never rest content with lack of knowledge; on the contrary, it is from our discontent with ignorance that the passion of faith stems.

This subjective definition of being a Christian prevents us from going into the byway of erudition, or being overwhelmed by intellectual anxiety. Indeed the quest for erudition is the antithesis of faith, turning the individual into a collector of bits of information, rather than a true believer. Faith is a matter of subjective decision, not objective knowledge.

LOVING YOURSELF

———————◆———————

from *Works of Love* (1847)

The statement, 'You should love your neighbour as yourself' presupposes that people love themselves. Thus Christianity is not free from presuppositions, as some philosophies are. And its main presupposition is not at all flattering.

Do we dare deny the presupposition of Christianity? On the other hand, could anyone imagine Christianity denying what worldly wisdom unanimously teaches, that people love themselves best? There is a paradox here: it appears that Christianity is honouring self-love; and yet the intention of Christianity is to strip away our selfishness. This selfishness consists of loving myself; but if I must love my neighbour as myself, then the commandment seems to break this self-love apart – and breaks me with it. The little phrase 'as yourself' is so easy to say, yet all eternity is contained in it. If the commandment did not contain this phrase, but was expressed in some other way, it would not be able to master my self-love. This phrase 'as yourself' is like an arrow which is aimed straight, with the unswerving accuracy of eternity, at my most secret hiding-place, that place where I love myself. It does not allow self-love any escape; it does not leave any loop-hole. How strange! Long and wise speeches could be made about how people should love their neighbours; and then, after all the speeches had been heard, self-love could still find an excuse for itself, and escape. This is because the subject had not been completely exhausted; the alternatives had not been fully explored; something had been forgotten; or something else had not been accurately expressed.

But this 'as yourself'! No wrestler can get such a tight grip on his opponent as the phrase gets on selfishness; in its grip selfishness can hardly move. The phrase is so easy to understand that no one needs to puzzle over it. When selfishness wrestles with it, then selfishness realises that it is grappling with a stronger power. As Jacob limped after he had wrestled with God, so selfishness will limp when it has wrestled with this phrase. It does not teach me that I should not love myself; rather it teaches me the proper kind of self-love. How strange! What battle is so protracted, so terrible, so complicated, as the battle of self-love in its own defence? And yet Christianity decides everything with a single blow.... Christianity presupposes that you love yourself, and merely adds to this a word about loving your neighbour 'as yourself'. In this lies the difference between earth and heaven.

But would this really be the highest form of love? Would it not be possible to love another person better than yourself? We hear people talk like that from time to time; they speak with the enthusiasm of poets. Could it be true that Christianity refused to soar to such a high standard, because it wanted to appeal to simple, ordinary folk? Is Christianity in this sense a rather feeble religion, making very meagre demands? Does Christianity, in using the pedestrian term 'neighbour' show that it lacks the noble ambition of poets, who speak of a 'beloved' and a 'friend'? Certainly no poets have ever sung about loving your neighbour, any more than they have sung about loving the neighbour 'as yourself'. Should we despise Christianity? Or should we make a distinction between the love of which poets sing, and the love which Christianity commands? Should we humbly praise the sober realism of Christianity and its understanding of life? Should we honour it for being so firmly rooted in this earth? Does Christianity share the spirit of the old proverb: 'Love me little, love me long?'

No; such questions should be far from our minds. Christianity has far better answers to questions about love – about the nature and the expression of love – than any poet. The love which the poets praise is secretly self-love; and this explains its intoxicated notion about loving another person more than yourself. Earthly love is not eternal love. It is a beautiful image of the infinite; it is the highest earthly reflection of the eternal. That is why it contains an element of fantasy, and even entertains the fantastic idea that people can love one another more than God. This kind of foolishness pleases the poet beyond all measure; it is delicious to his ears, and inspires him to sing. But alas, Christianity teaches us that it is blasphemy.

And what is true of love is also true of friendship. Friendship, like love, is partial, in the sense that you are more friendly towards one person than another. Friendship and earthly love make distinctions between people. That is why we refer to the objects of love and friendship in terms of partiality, such as 'the beloved' and 'the friend' – we love some people above others. But the Christian teaching is to love the neighbour, the whole race, all people, even my enemies, making no exceptions, ignoring all feelings of partiality or dislike.

There is only One whom people, with the honesty of eternal love, can claim to love better than themselves: God. Therefore the commandment does not say, 'You shall love God as yourself;' but it says, 'You shall love the Lord your God with all your heart and with all your soul and with all your mind.' I must love God in unconditional obedience, and love him in adoration. It would be utterly ungodly if I dared to love myself in this way, or dared to love another person in this way.

Imagine a friend begs me for something which in my honest love for him, I consider would harm him. It would be wrong to express my love for him by acquiescing in his wish; true love demands that I should deny his wish. But I must love God with total obedience, even if the demands he makes on me might seem to be harmful to me – and even harmful to his interests. God's wisdom is incomparably more profound than my own; and God's providence is not answerable to my cleverness. I have to obey God in love. Another person, on the other hand, I must love only as I love myself; and that is the highest form of love between one person and another. If I can discern my friend's interests better than he can, and if I acquiesce in his harmful wishes, I cannot excuse myself by saying that I was obedient to him. If it were right to acquiesce in my friend's harmful wishes, then I could properly speak of loving that friend more than I love myself. Such love would consist in obediently doing whatever he asked; and in doing it with adoration, because he wished it. But I have no right to do this; I am responsible for my friend, just as my friend is responsible for me.

THE ANATOMY OF DESPAIR

from *Sickness Unto Death* (1848–9)

The concept of sickness unto death must be understood in a peculiar sense. Literally it means sickness whose outcome is death. So we speak of terminal sickness as synonymous with sickness unto death. In this sense despair cannot be called sickness unto death. Yet in the Christian understanding, death in the bodily sense is a transition into life. Thus from a Christian standpoint there is no earthly, bodily sickness unto death. Death is the final phase of a terminal illness, but death itself is not final. If in this strict Christian sense we are to speak of a sickness unto death, it must be a sickness in which the final outcome is death, and death is final. And this is precisely what is meant by despair.

There is another and even more definite sense in which despair is sickness unto death. It is very far from being the case that, literally speaking, one dies of despair, or that despair ends with bodily death. On the contrary, the torment of despair is precisely this: that one is unable to die. To be in despair is to struggle with death, and yet not die; and at the same time, to have no hope of life. The hopelessness of despair is that even the last hope, death, is not available. When death is the greatest danger, I hope for life; but when I become acquainted with an even more dreadful danger, I hope for death. So when the danger is so great that death itself has become my hope, despair is the condition of not being able to die.

Despair is thus an agonising contradiction. It is a sickness of the self which causes the victim to die, and yet not to die; to suffer a continuing death in life. Dying means that it is all over; but the death of despair is to experience death without end. If for a single instant this experience is possible, it is tantamount to experiencing it forever. If I might die of despair as the body dies of a physical sickness, then the eternal soul – the self – must in this sense also be capable of dying. But this is an impossibility; the dying of despair lives continually. The despairing person cannot die. Just as a dagger cannot slay thoughts, despair cannot consume the eternal soul, the self, which is the place of despair. The worm of despair never dies, and the fire of despair is never quenched.

Yet despair is self-consuming; it is an impotent self-consumption in which the will is paralysed. In this paralysis those in despair are not able to do what they most want: to consume themselves. In this way despair is raised to a higher potency: the hot excitement, the cold fire, the gnawing canker, whose movement is constantly inward, deeper and deeper. There is no comfort to those in despair that their despair does not destroy the self; on the contrary, this apparent comfort is the real torment, keeping the pain alive, and making life continually painful. They despair because the self is not destroyed; they cannot get rid of themselves, and become nothing. This is why the fever of this sickness – this sickness of the self – never ceases to rise.

Those in despair appear to be in despair over something. But this appearance only lasts for an instant. That same instant the true nature of despair manifests itself; despair makes itself plain. Those in despair of something are really in despair of themselves, and wish to be rid of themselves. So the ambitious man, whose eyes are set on some great position of leadership, may fall into despair when he does not attain this position. But this signifies something else, that precisely because he did not attain this position, he now cannot endure himself. So he is not in despair over his failure, but over himself....

In fact to despair over something is not yet properly to despair. It is the beginning of despair; it is as if the physician says of a sickness that it has not yet come out. The next stage is for despair to come out, to declare itself.... If I am in despair I desperately want to be myself. But if I desperately want to be myself, I will not want to get rid of self. Or so it

seems. Looking more closely, one perceives a contradiction. That self which I desperately want to be, is a
self which I am not; if I wanted to be my true self, I
would not be in despair. What I really want is to tear
myself away from the Power which created that self.
Despite my despair, I am unable to do this; despite all
my efforts, that Power is too strong, and compels me
to be the self which I do not want to be. I desperately
want to be rid of the self that I am, in order to be the
self which I choose. To be the self which I choose
would be wonderful or at least so it seems, but to be
the self which I do not wish to be is my torment.
Despair is in truth the condition of being unable to
get rid of myself.

Socrates proved the immortality of the soul from
the fact that sickness of the soul (which may be called
sin) does not consume the soul, as sickness of the
body consumes the body. By extension we can say
that, because despair does not consume the self,
despair is the ultimate contradiction. If the human
frame did not contain an eternal soul, a self, humans
would not be capable of despair. Equally if despair
could consume the self, there would still be no
despair.

Thus it is that despair, this sickness of the self, is
the sickness unto death. In one sense those in despair
are mortally ill. In a quite different sense we can say
that the sickness has attacked the noblest part, the

soul; and for this reason it cannot be mortal. Death is not the last phase of despair; yet despair is death. To be released from this sickness is impossible, for the sickness and its torment consists in not being able to die.

This is an anatomy of despair. Those in despair may delude themselves that they do not really suffer the sickness unto death; indeed this self-delusion is quite common. But ultimately eternal truth will make things clear; it will reveal despair for what it is. Then those in despair will realise the nature of their torment, that they cannot get rid of themselves. Self-delusion will be shattered.

To have a self, to be a self, is the greatest gift of eternity to the human being. But it is also eternity's greatest demand.

REFLECTIONS ON FREEDOM

from *The Journal* (1850–54)

People believe that their freedom of choice enables them to take time, and to think matters over seriously. What a miserable anti-climax! 'Seriousness' implies choosing God at once and above all. In that way the notion of freedom of choice becomes a theological phantom, which raises unanswerable questions. If God is almighty and omniscient, how can people truly be free in their choices? If people choose God, and thereby submit to his will, do they lose their freedom of choice? Is freedom a gift from God in which humans should take delight, or a responsibility which humans cannot bear?

This is all a confusion. What matters is not freedom of choice, but the act of choosing. By concentrating on freedom of choice, we lost both freedom and choice. And they cannot be recovered through theological thought. The gift of choice – the true freedom – can only be recovered by first recognising that it has been lost.

The gift of choice, of freedom, is the most tremendous gift that has been granted to humanity. If you desire to love and preserve it, there is only one way: you must immediately, unconditionally and in total submission give it back to God – and give yourself as well. Naturally the gift is so tremendous that you want to keep hold of it. But if you yield to this temptation, and look with egotistical desire upon freedom of choice, you will lose your freedom. And your punishment will be this: you will be utterly confused, taking pride in an illusion. Freedom of choice which is not exercised in favour of God is not freedom at all. You will grow ill, because freedom of choice will become an obsession. You will be like a rich man who imagines he is so poor that he cannot feed himself, and so dies of hunger. In wanting to clasp freedom of choice to yourself, you will sense you are losing it. Perhaps finally you will grieve deeply enough at this loss, and do what is truly required.

* * *

Ideally it is right that every person should have freedom of conscience, belief, and so on. But what then? Where are the people spiritually strong enough to use that freedom – who are really capable of standing absolutely alone before God?

The idea that people should be free of all law and constraint, because they are essentially good, is both weak-minded and dangerous. People need a degree of constraint, especially in matters of great concern. If all constraint is removed, the mass of humankind will either cease to be anything at all, or fall under the power of demagogues and their partners....

The great spiritual figures of the past attained their stature by having to face every possible obstacle and constraint – and overcoming them. If the constraints had not been there, they would never have become what they became.

People want to do away with all constraint, and thus attain spiritual stature without effort. This is like doing away with cannon, powder and bayonet, and wanting to be a brave soldier. In order to be sure that conscience, and conscience alone determines your life (and not laziness, caprice, confusion or folly), it is necessary to have opposition and constraint. Conscience is such a fine element within the self that it is necessary to have the very finest filters in order to discover it. But once it is truly found, and distinguished from all other influences, then external constraint can be discarded.

Those who can really stand alone in the world, only taking counsel from conscience – they are the true heroes.

GOD AND HUMANITY

from *The Unchangeableness of God* (1855)

God is unchangeable. In his omnipotence he created this visible world; and he made himself invisible. He clothed himself in this visible world as if it were a garment. He changes it as if he were shifting the position of a garment for greater comfort; but he himself remains unchanged. In this world he is present everywhere at every moment. He is like an omniscient guard, watching all things and all people, but seen by no one. Every event, from the birth of a sparrow to the birth of a saviour, commands his complete attention. In each moment every outcome is possible, because he is almighty. He is constantly alert, able to change everything in an instant. He can alter people's opinions and their judgments; he can raise some people up, and put others down. He can change all, while he himself remains unchanged.

The external world may seem for a time to be stable; but in truth it is in a constant state of flux. Whether this flux is rapid or slow, God is untouched within himself. No change can affect him, not even the shadow of change. He is the source of all light, shining with perfect clarity. Indeed this is precisely why he remains unchanged: perfection cannot be altered; clarity of light, which has no trace of dimness in itself, cannot be touched by dimness. With people it is not like that. We are not perfectly clear, and for this reason we are subject to change; now something becomes clearer in us, and now something is dimmed, and hence we are changed. The shadow of these changes glides over us to alter us, and change takes place. The light that shines within each one of us is constantly altering its brightness. These thoughts are terrifying. We shake with fear. Yet surely they should be comforting. We frequently complain of the unreliability of people, and of all temporal things. So it is a consolation that we can rely totally on God.

But first and foremost you must ask yourself whether you have a relationship with God. Do you earnestly and sincerely strive to understand what God's will for you may be? Do you realise that God does have a purpose for you, and wants you to understand what the purpose may be? Or do you live your life in such a way that such questions never cross your mind? How terrifying it must be for you to think that God is eternally unchangeable! At some time, sooner or later, you must come into collision with his immutable will. God wants you to acknowledge and seek to understand his will, because he desires your well-being. But if you try to oppose his will, you will eventually be crushed.

In the second place, once you have entered a relationship with God, you must ask yourself whether it is a good relationship. Have you submitted your will, totally and unconditionally, to his will? Do you want his wishes to become your wishes, his thoughts to become your thoughts? If not, how terrifying it must be for you to think that God is eternally unchangeable! In this regard, consider what it means to be at odds with another person. Perhaps you are stronger, and console yourself with the thought that you can compel the other person into accepting your views. If the other person is stronger, you might think you have more powers of endurance. If you are at odds not just with one person, but with an entire generation, you might say to yourself: seventy years is no eternity. Yet when you are at odds with one who is eternally unchangeable, when the disagreement is set to last for all eternity, that is truly terrifying!...

In truth your will, my will, and the wills of all the people around us, are not entirely in harmony with God's will. Nevertheless matters take their course in the hurly-burly of the so-called actual world. It seems as if God is not paying attention. A righteous person – if such a person exists – contemplating this world (which the Scriptures say is dominated by evil), would feel disheartened, because God does not seem to be making his presence felt. But do you therefore conclude that God has undergone some change? Or if you are certain that he remains unchangeable, do you feel terrified that he does not assert his power more strongly? To me it does not seem so.

Consider these two pictures, and tell me which is more terrible. The first picture is of one who is infinitely stronger than any creature, and who grows tired of being mocked. In his power he rises up against those who scorn him, and metes out the most dreadful punishments. This is surely a terrifying image. The second picture is of one who is infinitely powerful and eternally unchangeable, and who sits still; he sees everything, but he does not alter his expression. It is almost as if he does not exist. As a result those who are dishonest achieve success and power; those who are most cruel are victorious; and those who would prefer to act honestly and justly feel they are compelled to compromise – while at the same time complaining to God for his inaction. Thus God – infinitely powerful and eternally unchangeable – is being held in contempt. This is surely an even more terrifying image. And why, do you think, is he so quiet? Because he knows that within himself he is eternally unchangeable. Any being that was not so eternally sure of himself could not keep so still, but would rise in his strength. Only one who is eternally immutable can remain so passive.

God gives people time. And he can afford to give people time, because he has all eternity and is eternally unchangeable. He gives time quite intentionally. Ultimately in eternity an account will be made, from which nothing is left out, not even a single one of the improper words that were spoken. And God remains eternally unchanged. And yet it is also perhaps en expression of his mercy that he gives people time – time for conversion and improvement. But how terrible if the time is not used for that purpose! If people are so foolish and frivolous as to waste the time he gives, it would be better if he punished them straight away; there would then be fewer wrongs to punish....

There is, therefore, fear and trembling, for us frivolous and unstable human beings, in the thought of God's unchangeableness. Consider it carefully! Whether or not God makes himself immediately felt in our lives, he is eternally unchangeable. You perhaps once pledged yourself to him, promising to serve; but in the course of time you have changed, and now rarely think about him. Now you have grown older you think you have better things than God to occupy your mind. Or perhaps you have different notions about God, and think that he does not concern himself with the trifles of your life – you regard such an idea as childish. In any case you have virtually forgotten about your pledge, and forgotten how you thought it would affect your life. You may have forgotten, but he has forgotten nothing. He is eternally unchangeable. To imagine that anything is insignificant to God, or that God forgets things, is the inverted childishness of mature years....

Compare God, who is eternally unchangeable, with the human heart. Your heart is hidden in the deepest recesses of your personality, unknown to others. But that is the least of it; your heart is almost unknown to yourself. After you have lived for a few years into middle-age, the human heart becomes almost a burial-plot. Within the heart all sorts of things are buried in forgetfulness: promises, intentions, resolutions, entire plans and fragments of plans, and God knows what else. Indeed we humans use the phrase 'God knows what', without thinking what we are saying. We say it in a frivolous, even cynical, spirit. And yet it is horribly true that God does know what, down to the last detail. He knows what you have forgotten; he recalls accurately what your memory has distorted, because to him the past is present. He does not remember things as if they were some time ago; he remembers them as if they were today. He knows whether you ever spoke to him about your wishes, intentions and resolutions – because he is eternally unchanged and unchangeable. You may feel burdened by the knowledge that other people can recall negative things about your past. But their memories are faulty; and, besides, they cannot last forever – some time you can expect to be freed from them.

But you can never be freed from the memories of the one who is omniscient and unchangeable....

Yet there is also peace and happiness in this thought. A time comes when you feel weary of human inconstancy, weary of unending change and weary too of your own inconstancy. You wish to find a place where you can rest your weary head, your weary thoughts, and your weary spirit, so that you might be refreshed. And in the unchangeableness of God there is indeed rest and refreshment. Let this unchangeableness serve you, according to his will; let it care for you, both now and eternally. Submit to its discipline, so that your selfish will dies away; and it is from this submission that true change will come. The sooner you act, the better. Your will may resist; but think how foolish it is for your will to be at odds with eternal immutability. So be like a child in relation to a powerful adult will, to which the only response is obedience. When you submit to God's unchangeable will, and accept his discipline, you renounce inconstancy, changeableness, caprice and self-will. The result is that you will find greater and greater inner peace, strengthened security. You will experience the unchangeableness of God as a wonderful blessing.

Looked at in this way, who can doubt that the thought of God's unchangeableness is a blessed thought? But ensure that you attain a state of mind in which you can rest happily in this immutability. People in this state of mind speak about God as they would about a happy home. They say: 'My home is eternally secure; I rest in the unchangeableness of God.' This is a rest from which no one can disturb you – except you yourself. If you become completely obedient – and if your obedience is constant and unchanging – you will be able to release yourself into God's care.

FURTHER READING

All the works mentioned in this book appear, in recent translations, in the Penguin Classics series. Earlier translations, which remain highly respected, were made by Walter Lowrie. Most of these are not in print, but *A Kierkegaard Anthology*, edited by Robert Bretall, includes extensive extracts, and is published by the Princeton University Press.

PHILOSOPHERS OF THE SPIRIT

Some other titles in this series

Hildegard

A twelfth-century German mystic, Hildegard is being re-discovered today both as a musical composer and as a spiritual prophet of the environmental movement. In her visions she saw the Logos – the Word of God – in all living things. And she saw that human beings can find inner peace and tranquillity only if they recognise their spiritual unity with all animals and plants.

As this new collection of her writings reveals, her insights into the human psyche and its relationship with the whole created order seem astonishingly modern.

Pascal

Blaise Pascal, writing in the seventeenth century, was both scientist and philosopher. He found a way of combining rational and religious scepticism. In penetrating and often witty epigrams, he saw clearly the paradoxes and dilemmas of the human condition., and he concluded that gambling on faith was the only way of resolving them.

Socrates

Socrates, the great teacher of ancient Athens, was a philosopher and a mystic – and a notorious de-bunker. He wrote nothing down, and our only reliable witness is the works of his disciple Plato. Condemned to death by his enemies, the account of his final hours is one of the highlights of classical literaure.